# Transitioning
## Out of Darkness

Shalisha Owens

Copyright © 2018 by Shalisa Owens

All rights reserved. No part of this publication may be reproduced, distributed, or transmitted in any form or by any means, including photocopying, recording, or other electronic or mechanical methods, without the prior written permission of the publisher, except in the case of brief quotations embodied in critical reviews and certain other noncommercial uses permitted by copyright law.

ISBN: 978-1-7326934-0-1

Liberation's Publishing LLC
West Point, Mississippi
www.liberationspublishing.com

# Rise

Why are you sitting in despair,

Why are you so dismayed,

Why are you living as though you are a fatherless child,

wondering from place to place,

lost staring in a daze

# Contents

Poetic Meditation ................................................................. 3
   Daughter Of The Call ...................................................... 3

Deeper Understanding ......................................................... 5
   Knowing Who You Are ..................................................... 5

Poetic Inspiration ................................................................. 7
   This Life .............................................................................. 7

Words of inspiration ............................................................ 10
   Stand Firm ........................................................................ 10

Poetic Meditation ............................................................... 11
   Woman Thou Woman ..................................................... 11

Deeper Understanding ....................................................... 13
   Woman Thou Woman ..................................................... 13

Poetic Inspiration ............................................................... 16
   Rise My Child ................................................................... 16

Poetic Meditation ............................................................... 17

| | |
|---|---|
| Emptiness | 17 |
| Deeper Understanding | 18 |
| Poetic Meditation | 21 |
|    Bitterness | 21 |
| Deeper Understanding | 22 |
|    A Heart of Bitterness | 22 |
| Poetic Meditation | 25 |
|    My Inner Being | 25 |
| Deeper Understanding | 26 |
|    The Inner Man | 26 |
| Poetic Meditation | 29 |
|    Who Am I? | 29 |
| Deeper Understanding | 31 |
|    Who Am I | 31 |
| Poetic inspiration | 34 |
|    Princess Cut Diamonds | 34 |
| Poetic Meditation | 37 |

| | |
|---|---|
| My Daughter | 37 |
| Deeper understanding | 39 |
| My Daughter | 39 |
| Poetic meditation | 43 |
| The Other Me | 43 |
| Deeper understanding | 44 |
| The Other Me | 44 |
| Words of inspiration | 47 |
| Adversity | 47 |
| Poetic Mediation | 49 |
| Life | 49 |
| A deeper Understanding | 50 |
| Life | 50 |
| Poetic Meditation | 53 |
| My Child | 53 |
| Deeper Understanding | 55 |
| About the Author | 59 |

Shalisha Owens..................................................................59

There is a certain type of existence

A living being with no emotions or understanding

Living from day to day with no attachment to anything

Detached from the world and the spirit

Bound and confused not knowing anything truly

Spinning in circles with no sense of directing, but grasping and latching on to any close interaction

Not truly understanding the depth of thing

Always watching others in amazement as

They rejoice and give God Praise

-Shalisha Owens

# POETIC MEDITATION

## Daughter Of The Call

Daughter of the call...Know your worth. God has called you to a place of personal worship

Daughter of the call...Know your place. You are not like those in the world who are lost and complacent

Daughter of the call...Know your potential and the power God has given you

Daughter of the call...Stand bold and tall... AND walk with your God given authority

Daughter of the call...Be humble and meek...AND seek God for your inner and outer beauty needs

Daughter of the call...Speak life into your family and your destiny

Daughter of the call...Be mindful and cautious on how you speak and critique

Daughter of the call...don't be hypnotized by this world's beauty and techniques

Daughter of the call...Don't fall into this world's lies and deceit

Daughter of the call...Be graceful and merciful to all those that come to you with a need

Daughter of the call...Live your life like Christ so that whoever you meet will know that you are a child of the King

Daughter of the call...Be that Proverbs 31 woman that God has called you to be

"ye then be risen with Christ, seek those things which are above, where Christ sitteth on the right hand of God. ²Set your affection on things above, not on things on the earth. ³For ye are dead, and your life is hid with Christ in God." Colossians 3:1-3(NKJV)

# DEEPER UNDERSTANDING
## Knowing Who You Are

Knowing who you are is imperative to knowing where you are going. When you are confused about whom you are your outlook on life is cloudy and you are easily manipulated into a way of being that is contrary to true identity.

When you have no idea of your identity and purpose you float from home to home like an orphan with no parental guidance. This causes a lack of spiritual growth and you began to carry characteristic traits of this confuse adulterated world.

When you don't know where you are going, you are tossed around like a boat with no anchor, bouncing from place to place never taking root, and never arriving a specified location.

So many Christians struggle with identity, "Why was I created? Where am I going?" They blindly move through life pretending to be something they are not. They have not sought God nor his vision for their lives. They are running with no purpose.

Decide today to accept who you are, a child of God. Seek his Kingdom and it's righteousness because your identity is hid in Christ. In him you will find purpose and reason for existing. You will know the way of an effectual Christian!

> "ye then be risen with Christ, seek those things which are above, where Christ sitteth on the right hand of God. ²Set your affection on things above, not on things on the earth. ³For ye are dead, and your life is hid with Christ in God." Colossians 3:1-3(NKJV)

# POETIC INSPIRATION

## *This Life*

There will be times we all face obstacle, and it is within those times that we must lean on our Heavenly Father. This is a part of our maturing process. It is a time of the word being enhanced in our life, by receiving and accepting the word. The word of God opens us up to the will of God for our lives, his desires toward us.

In those times the test will throw you forward or leave you at a standstill. Spiritual maturity as a woman of GOD means the test throw you forward. You realize that with your enhancement comes Great Authority and Responsibilities. The higher you grow in Christ the more responsibilities you will have. Learning to be submissive to Christ is essential as well as the need to overcome those obstacles through grace and obedience. Being his child is a hard task that brings so many positive and fulfilling attributes.

Think about it, Eternal life. WOW! A place and life with no pain or deceit just peace; ACTUALLY LIVING PEACE!!!

## Self-Reflection

"ye then be risen with Christ, seek those things which are above, where Christ sitteth on the right hand of God. ²Set your affection on things above, not on things on the earth. ³For ye are dead, and your life is hid with Christ in God." Colossians 3:1-3(NKJV)

# WORDS OF INSPIRATION

## Stand Firm

Hold fast to the word,

Stand firm in the faith,

Be all that God has called you to be.

Speak victory and claim power over defeat,

And know that He who has called you,

Will give you the power,

To beat team defeat.

# POETIC MEDITATION

## Woman Thou Woman

Woman thou woman, TAKE YOUR PLACE

Walk in the AUTHORITY that I have given you.

Take to your prayer closet

Reach for your cloth and kneel before me

SEEK my face and extend your hands towards me

Trust me and let me lead thee to that next level of destiny

Turn your eyes toward me

Deny thy own understanding and allow me to anoint thee

I will give you my supernatural strength that comes only from me.

My anointing will be so POWERFUL and INDULGING that the flow will spread even to though enemies.

That they will be unable to walk in your presence without feeling the flow of me

Woman thou woman take Your PLACE

³ The aged women likewise, that they be in behaviour as becometh holiness, not false accusers, not given to much wine, teachers of good things; ⁴ That they may teach the young women to be sober, to love their husbands, to love their children, ⁵ To be discreet, chaste, keepers at home, good, obedient to their own husbands, that the word of God be not blasphemed. Titus 2:3-5 (NKJV)

# DEEPER UNDERSTANDING

## *Woman Thou Woman*

A woman is the glue that holds the family together. She is the secret weapon that God has put on the scene to go into war for what others can't see. She's that silent compass that helps point her husband and children in the right direction. Her peace and inner glow helps to spread throughout her home keeping all things calm.

When the woman is not in her rightful place....her home falls apart...and when glue is not working properly it tends to not hold the pieces together...So, in other words...Your marriage begins to break down, your children begins to fall off...Things begin to break and roll away into different directions.

Self-Reflection

---

[3] The aged women likewise, that they be in behaviour as becometh holiness, not false accusers, not given to much wine, teachers of good things; [4] That they may teach the young women to be sober, to love their husbands, to love their children, [5] To be discreet, chaste, keepers at home, good, obedient to their own husbands, that the word of God be not blasphemed. Titus 2:3-5 (NKJV)

# POETIC INSPIRATION

## Rise My Child

Have I not instructed you in my word on how to defeat the enemy. Have I not sent the Holy Spirit to help lead and guide you?

I have given you each and everything you need to live a life of victory. I have shown you my great works of the past and even in your days to come.

You are equipped to fight each and every fight that comes up against you. So child, my child, my seed, my royal priesthood, you are no longer fatherless you have been adopted into the Highest of Highest of Royalty.

So RISE, Stand Tall, Be strong and walk in the Power that has been given to you. RISE, I say, RISE I beseech you to RISE and be all that I created you to be.

RISE my child, RISE!!!!

# POETIC MEDITATION

## *Emptiness*

My heart longs for intimacy.

There is an emptiness longing in my soul.

There is a part of me that screams out, but only heard deep within my personal hole.

I yearn for fullness, but that fullness has to start within.

My inner desire is to be held and have a full life without sin.

That intimacy I'm yearning for only comes from the touch of my master's hand.

Because all the other Earthly desires only been pleasing for a little while.

His love and his compassion fulfill my emptiness; leading me to fullness from his light that now dwells within. I am so glad to know that all I have been seeking for, lies within Him.

> [9] **For in him dwelleth all the fulness of the Godhead bodily.**
> [10] **And ye are complete in him, which is the head of all principality and power. Colossian 2:9-10 (NKJV)**

# DEEPER UNDERSTANDING

Emptiness is an issue that so many people face on a day to day basis. Living and existing on the outside but on the inside crying or dying. Too many times people try to fill spots of emptiness with Earthly things that please them temporarily

This is a being that recognizes their place of hurt, but the spirit reveals the true fulfillment that they need which is the heavenly father.

[9] For in him dwelleth all the fulness of the Godhead bodily.
[10] And ye are complete in him, which is the head of all principality and power. Colossian 2:9-10 (NKJV)

Self-Reflection

⁹ For in him dwelleth all the fulness of the Godhead bodily.
¹⁰ And ye are complete in him, which is the head of all principality and power. Colossian 2:9-10 (NKJV)

# POETIC MEDITATION

## Bitterness

Bitterness rots your soul and turns your heart to black mold.

It slowly eats at your flesh and not allows you any peace or rest.

It's a pest that latches on and eats on your sensual ness.

It slowly deteriorates you from the inside out leaving

you dry and wrinkle, with so many signs of doubt.

No hope, no life, no happiness, but

the humiliation of anger and un-restfulness.

Bitterness is a base that brings no living peace,

but has a key that opens up to evil deeds.

The distress, the strain and the uneasiness makes one bitter with envious.

Bitterness is a sickness that slowly kills unless

released and willing to be healed.

**31 Let all bitterness, wrath, anger, clamor, and evil speaking be put away from you, with all malice. 32 And be kind to one another, tenderhearted, forgiving one another, even as God in Christ forgave you Ephesians 4:31-32 (NKJV)**

# DEEPER UNDERSTANDING

## *A Heart of Bitterness*

Bitterness illustrates a broken and unforgiving being. A being that is boiling with hatred and evil deeds.

The being is flipped inside out and is deteriorating from within. Bitterness slowly kills and allows no peace which means the Holy Spirit is hindered from working within. So as Children of God we should not allow our hurts and pain to destroy us and separate us from the love of God.

How can we say I love God but hate your brother and sister you see every day. The word says you are a liar so as children of God we must forgive because God has forgiven us

**31 Let all bitterness, wrath, anger, clamor, and evil speaking be put away from you, with all malice. 32 And be kind to one another, tenderhearted, forgiving one another, even as God in Christ forgave you Ephesians 4:31-32 (NKJV)**

Self-Reflection

31 Let all bitterness, wrath, anger, clamor, and evil speaking be put away from you, with all malice. 32 And be kind to one another, tenderhearted, forgiving one another, even as God in Christ forgave you Ephesians 4:31-32 (NKJV)

# POETIC MEDITATION

## My Inner Being

My inner being is my inner most beliefs that are unseen.

My inner being is the real me hidden from all discreet.

My inner being speaks of my desires and my outermost dreams.

My inner being is what I thrive off to reach my dreams.

My inner being is the true person within me.

My inner being is a second human being underneath me.

My inner being helps to complete me.

My inner being is a true spirit that lives within me.

**Behold, You desire truth in the inward parts, And in the hidden part You will make me to know wisdom. Psalm 51:6 (NKJV)**

# DEEPER UNDERSTANDING

## *The Inner Man*

My inner being is acknowledging that there is an inner man, and that the inner man holds deep

secrets from deep within. No matter what you see on the outside everyone has a

second human being underneath. The inner being is the true being that shows the

characteristics traits of the person you see.

> **Behold, You desire truth in the inward parts, And in the hidden part You will make me to know wisdom. Psalm 51:6 (NKJV)**

Self-Reflection

Behold, You desire truth in the inward parts, And in the hidden part You will make me to know wisdom. Psalm 51:6 (NKJV)

# POETIC MEDITATION

## Who Am I?

Who am I? Am I truly me or am I who you want me to be?

Who am I? Am I a flower blowing in your wind or am I a flower blowing in my own wind?

Who am I? Am I who you imagine me to be or am I who I want to be?

Who am I? Am I who God made me or am I who you molded me to be?

Who am I? Am I truly me or a disguised human being with iniquities?

Who am I? Am I just a shell with a heart with no feelings or no remorse?

Who am I? Am I a cloud of smoke that blows within the drift of an egg yolk?

Who am I? Am I considered your trash that you discard when you have had enough or your recyclable item that you use over and over again when it's convenient for you?

So again, WHO AM I?

I am neither of those things you want me to be. BUT I am who God made me.

I am a human being with my own personality and unique peaks.

I am a vessel full of love and remorse.

I AM ME the MAGNIFICENT ME! THE ONE AND ONLY ME!

I AM who God made me to BE!

> For we are His workmanship, created in Christ Jesus for good works, which God prepared beforehand that we should walk in them. Ephesians 2:10 (NKJV)

# DEEPER UNDERSTANDING

## Who Am I

A person that has compromised their character to please others. They have no identity in Christ and have no problem with watching you live contrary to the word of God. It speaks to a person that is in a dangerous place of struggling between two worlds.

> For we are His workmanship, created in Christ Jesus for good works, which God prepared beforehand that we should walk in them. Ephesians 2:10 (NKJV)

Self-Reflection

For we are His workmanship, created in Christ Jesus for good works, which God prepared beforehand that we should walk in them. Ephesians 2:10 (NKJV)

# POETIC INSPIRATION

## *Princess Cut Diamonds*

We are all precious diamonds retrieved from the roughest places of life. In spite of our environments and different life situations, we are all still precious jewels. We all have issues and things we are not pleased with. But because of our heavenly Father's ability as a gem cutter, He knows how and what to use to get rid of those things not of him. In the midst of his sawing, grinding and sanding HE smoothed out all those rough spots and grazes us to be more like him.

This is a hurtful process. But we have to remember he's the King of ALL King's. He desire's his precious jewels to be cut perfectly and unique. We are no longer ordinary jewels; we are HIS DIAMONDS that he has rescued out of despair.

Because of his love and compassion he took the necessary time to turn a plain gem into a PRINCESS CUT diamond with a unique shape and fixture that is pleasing to only him. Through his sawing, grinding, and sanding he had a vision. And in his vision HE knew what he was shaping each and every one of us out to be. He was shaping us out to be HIS PRINCESS'S and Ladies of Royalty!!! We were adopted into a Royal family and given the Authority and Power that extends into our families. So, as Princesses and Daughters of the King walk with BOLDNESS and DECLARE VICTORY!!!!!

# POETIC MEDITATION

## *My Daughter*

I see the storms raging in your life

I see the chaos within your home

I see the despair in your heart

I see the trouble on your job

I see your body racking in pain

I know the headaches of your finances

I tell you, If you will only trust me, things will get much better

Your heart despair

Throw them all on me, and I will make your burdens lighter

I will give you a place of rest

I love you, and I want the best for you

Do not feel abandoned or overwhelmed

I am here...

I hear your cries and your deep desires

BUT!!! JUST TRUST ME!!

If you will throw me all your chaos and all your worries

I will give you rest

I promise

Just test me and see

> 28 Come to Me, all you who labor and are heavy laden, and I will give you rest. 29 Take My yoke upon you and learn from Me, for I am [a]gentle and lowly in heart, and you will find rest for your souls. 30 For My yoke is easy and My burden is light." Matthews 11:28-30

# DEEPER UNDERSTANDING

## *My Daughter*

My daughter is an encouraging poem. This poem is informing the daughters of God that he hears and he knows everything. The author is wanting her to know that she is not alone. If she cast her cares on God he will give her peace and rest.

> 28 Come to Me, all you who labor and are heavy laden, and I will give you rest. 29 Take My yoke upon you and learn from Me, for I am [a]gentle and lowly in heart, and you will find rest for your souls. 30 For My yoke is easy and My burden is light." Matthews 11:28-30

Self-Reflection

28 Come to Me, all you who labor and are heavy laden, and I will give you rest. 29 Take My yoke upon you and learn from Me, for I am [a]gentle and lowly in heart, and you will find rest for your souls. 30 For My yoke is easy and My burden is light." Matthews 11:28-30

# POETIC MEDITATION

## The Other Me

The other me is the woman behind the scenes.

The other me is the woman broken and bruised with iniquities

The other me is a bitter and scornful lady with a fake meet and greet

The other me is the woman of defeat

The other me is a woman with a fake identity

The other me is the woman that many people don't see

The other me is that woman who needs a true identity

Is it you?

Is it Me?

Who is she?

The other me

> To console those who mourn in Zion, To give them beauty for ashes, The oil of joy for mourning, The garment of praise for the spirit of heaviness; Isaiah 61:3 (NKJV)

# DEEPER UNDERSTANDING

## The Other Me

The other me addresses the things that go on deep within a broken human being. A person that we see in church, on our jobs, in the stores, and around our towns. This person is struggling with past pain and hurt. She is broken but she smiles and puts on as if everything is okay. This person can be anyone.

> To console those who mourn in Zion, To give them beauty for ashes, The oil of joy for mourning, The garment of praise for the spirit of heaviness; Isaiah 61:3 (NKJV)

Self-Reflection

To console those who mourn in Zion, To give them beauty for ashes, The oil of joy for mourning, The garment of praise for the spirit of heaviness; Isaiah 61:3 (NKJV)

# WORDS OF INSPIRATION

## Adversity

Standing in the middle of adversity,

Tests your character, tests your faith and

Test your ability to operate faithfully in the kingdom of God, while being tried in the furnace.

Standing in the middle of adversity,

Shows you who you really are, and who God really is.

# POETIC MEDIATION

## *Life*

Hard and unorganized.

Strange but yet so simple. Mean but yet so loving.

A place that can be sweet but yet so bitter.

Loving and unloving. LIFE! Is what you make it to be.

You can be tossed with every blowing wind or

you can be firm and stand strong through the storms.

You can be a tornado swirling out of control or

Better yet the sea with the waves gushing at peace. LIFE!

It's all what you make it to be.

**These things I have spoken to you, that in Me you may have peace. In the world you [a]will have tribulation; but be of good cheer, I have overcome the world." John 16:33(NKJV)**

# A DEEPER UNDERSTANDING

## *Life*

Life is very direct. It encourages you to stand in spite of your circumstances. Although, you may go through, our going through is exactly what it is

A GOING THROUGH.

We must learn to accept the good as well as the bad. As people we must NOT ALLOW our circumstances or situations to define us. We must remember God is in control and we are just passengers along for the ride.

**These things I have spoken to you, that in Me you may have peace. In the world you [a]will have tribulation; but be of good cheer, I have overcome the world." John 16:33(NKJV)**

Self-Reflection

These things I have spoken to you, that in Me you may have peace. In the world you [a]will have tribulation; but be of good cheer, I have overcome the world." John 16:33(NKJV)

# POETIC MEDITATION

## *My Child*

My child.....

Sunday after Sunday,

Wednesday after Wednesday,

Revival after Revival

You sit, you stare, and you murmur

As though you heard nothing at all

I call to you BUT you don't answer

I plead with you BUT you ignore me

I give you visions and dreams of what's to come BUT you don't seek me

My child....

I am calling you

I am constantly guiding you toward the things of me BUT you turn away

Don't be deceived by this world,

Don't be miss-lead by what you see.....

Your popularity means nothing to me......

Your fancy clothes don't move me......

Your expensive shoes don't excite me......

Child, O child, if you will only let me guide thee..... You can truly see how much better life can be......

The time is now, your anointing is high, and you're in the BEST place of your life....

Give me you!!!! I have so much more for you....

Don't be dismayed by what your so-called friends think........ BUT;

SURRENDER your life to me and I can guide thee to that next level of destiny.....

# DEEPER UNDERSTANDING

God is calling us to focus more on him. He is calling us to go deeper. Our society is so caught up in religion, rituals, fancy church clothes, and different church functions that we have forgotten about the true meaning of Christian. God is wanting to meet each and every need of ours, but we are NOT listening to the call.

## Self-Reflection

# ABOUT THE AUTHOR

*Shalisha Owens*

Shalisha Owens a native of Mississippi. I am a woman of color. I'm a mother, a wife, and a woman of God. Being a woman of color does not actually mean the color of my skin: It means the different elements of my life.

I began writing at a young age but never truly knew the purpose of my gift. As I matured and began to build a family, the cares of this world began to bring me down. During this time of my life I fought with depression, defeat, hurts, betrayal, and marital issues.

God began to reveal things to me on a level that I could not understand. He began to awake me throughout the wee hours with dreams, words, and sayings that were so powerful and indulging. I began to put everything in writing that he laid upon my heart. The desire and the need to write began to return, so strong. The things that he gave me began to minister to my past hurts and pain.

Writing is my outlet but it is also a ministry. It's a way for me to encourage those that have experienced, or is experiencing the same hurts. So, now I pray that the writings God gave me will help to encourage others.

www.ingramcontent.com/pod-product-compliance
Lightning Source LLC
Chambersburg PA
CBHW060342080526
44584CB00013B/883